Action From Interaction

Corey B. Pruitt

Action From Interaction
"The art and science of managing performance outcomes
through communication"
By
Corey Pruitt, MS, CMC, CPC

A Publication of
The National Human Communication Institute
Phoenix, Arizona

http://www.NHCIonline.com

Unattributed quotations are by Corey Pruitt

Editorial Staff: Angela Pruitt, Terri Plucker, Judy Bussemeier
Cover designed by: Corey Pruitt
Printed in the United States of America
Disclaimer: All references to "he", "him", "his" encompass both male and
female genders.

ISBN: 0-9830-9130-7
ISBN-13: 978-0-9830913-0-1
Library of Congress Control Number: 2010939476

Contents

Chapter 1

Powerful leaders are constantly asking, "How can I make sure I'm as effective as I can be? How do I continue to get unparalleled results from each of my staff members?" "How can I get more effective performance with fewer resources?" "Why does my staff do some of the things they do?"

Your job is changing all the time. It's a sign of the times:
- There's more to be done and fewer employees on your staff to get things done.
- Employees change jobs more frequently, leaving you in constant training mode.
- Your staff feel frazzled by the chaotic pace.
- The talent pool for the skills you need seems to be shallower than ever before.
- Your strong performers are uncommitted and lack loyalty.

And, you're wondering how to clear all these leadership hurdles to get the results you need.

While facing ever greater management challenges, how do today's managers and leaders motivate their staff to exert peak performance outcomes?

How are managers and leaders guiding their people in a new era of unequalled change and diversity when the management playing field is more challenging than ever before?

The old rules of management and supervision simply don't work with today's complex, multi-cultural and multi-generational workforce. That's why the most effective leaders in America now rely on one profitable and powerful management method to lead their teams to success. So, what's the method of leadership effectiveness today? It's called "Performance Communication."

Early in life I realized that most people, if given the opportunity, want to become better than they are. Most people, if given the chance, want to be great at something. I know very few people who wake up and say, "I want to be worse today than I was yesterday!"

Through years of coaching managers and leadership, as well as training thousands of individuals on the concept of communication and motivating others toward behavior change, I learned the crucial techniques and strategies that will influence positive and sustainable performance improvement.

"Deep within man dwell those slumbering powers; powers that would astonish him, that he never dreamed of possessing; forces that would revolutionize his life if aroused and put into action."
Orison Swett Marden

I discovered specific ways to influence increased performance in others; ways that aren't often expressed in any book, college business course or training program. However, these techniques are used by many influential leaders, managers, coaches, parents, counselors and a handful of companies. These techniques, methods and philosophies are drawn from industry, athletics, education and science.

Take the executive leader attempting to share his progressive company vision, but for some reason is not getting "buy in" from his managers. Or, the supervisor who constantly has to have "coaching sessions" with her staff regarding the same issue over and over. Similarly, the business owner yearning to grow his business but keeps hitting a barrier with his sales staff. The thread that runs through these scenarios and countless others is the lack of performance communication.

What is performance communication?

Performance communication is the art and science of using human communication skills and techniques to increase another person's performance. Put simply, how a leader (president, director, manager, supervisor, etc.) communicates with others will be a strong predictor of their performance output.

Communicate your way to phenomenal team results

You need expert performance communication techniques to ensure your staff fully devote their talents and become motivated in order to support their coworkers and associates through the toughest challenges. Through effective performance communication, you'll build loyalty and trust by making every team member feel valued, appreciated and understood. And you'll know exactly how to coach your underperformers, inspiring them to become strong contributors to assignments, projects and even company goals and outcomes.

Take your employees' skills to the next level through performance communication

Effective performance communication is vital to your leadership success. It's through performance communication that your most valued employees can realize their full potential and take their skills to the next level. Great talent is hard to find and harder to keep—and performance communication improves employee retention.

Solve repetitive problems you face as a leader

The practical communication methods and techniques you'll master in this book will immediately improve your effectiveness in dealing with recurring employee issues, excuses, burnout and so much more. Using the performance communication methods you'll learn, you'll put an end to badgering problems that have robbed you and your team of valuable time, resources, energy and outcomes.

Learn how you can adapt your approach for better results

One of the most perplexing jobs leaders face is getting team members with potential to take their skills to the next level. The secret to developing employees is performance communication, which is why you'll learn essential how-to's for becoming a strong performance communicator, plus tips for avoiding common communication pitfalls.

Coach a team of motivated, productive winners

With the expert performance communication tools and methods, you'll inspire your team to strive for excellence, not settle for mediocrity. What's more, you'll motivate them to peak performance through your management style so you don't have to worry about financial resources to spend.

Create high-energy, collaborative and performance inducing teams

Say goodbye to average performance and weakening morale! The performance communication skills you'll learn will help you establish a high-energy, positive environment that fosters teamwork, focused on results and a high level of self-motivated performance.

Boost performance through effective feedback

Effective feedback is the foundation of successful performance communication. That's why you'll learn an easy, step-by-step method for providing feedback to team members in a way that results in positive behavior change and growth, rather than anger, resentment and short-term performance outcomes.

Performance Phases

Before we dig too deep into the elements and methods that comprise performance communication, we must first take a look at the four phases of employee performance. These phases will give you a general guide as to where a leader (chief, director, manager, supervisor, etc) fits into the performance cycle.

There are four key criteria that span across each performance phase. These four key performance criteria are: Knowledge, Skill, Confidence, and Motivation. Here is a brief breakdown of each performance criteria:

Knowledge: the level of information, familiarity and understanding of company processes, procedures, norms and expectations.

Skill: the level of proficiency and competence for which the individual was hired as it relates to the company culture, norms and expectations.

Confidence: the level of internal belief about the certainty of success the employee has regarding his knowledge and skill as it relates to the company culture, norms and expectations.

Motivation: the level of internal drive the employee possess regarding specific job duties, functions and expectations within the company culture.

These four criteria drastically influence the performance outcome and impact each performance phase.

Phase I: Arrival Phase
Knowledge: low
Skill: low
Confidence: mid
Motivation: high

The arrival phase of performance is when an employee first walks through the door of your company. I call this the "I shined my shoes, wore my best tie, brushed my teeth" phase of the performance phases. First impressions are critical for both parties (the employee and the company) at this phase in impacting eventual performance. The "new" employee typically has high motivation during the Arrival Phase, and this high desire to perform well is the driving force that overrides the fear of having low knowledge and low skill.

The Arrival Phase typically lasts for the first one to two days on the job.

Phase II: Activation Phase
Knowledge: mid to high
Skill: mid to high
Confidence: mid to high
Motivation: high

The Activation Phase is typically known as "orientation and training." There are mounds of books on how to make this portion of the employee performance cycle successful. The focus of this book is not on this phase. However, it is imperative that this phase is conducted properly for long term performance outcomes. The Activation Phase can either be a breeding ground for breakdown or a source for success as it relates to impacting eventual performance.

The Activation Phase typically lasts from day two to day thirty on the job.

Phase III: Audition Phase
Knowledge: high
Skill: high
Confidence: high
Motivation: high

The Audition Phase is a practice run, a fitting, an audition of new information and skills. It is where the new employee puts into practice what they have learned and observed through the orientation and training that was provided. Notice that all four criteria are typically high at this point in the performance phases. This occurs because the employee knows what they are supposed to do and how they are supposed to do it successfully. This increase in knowledge and skill quickly raises the confidence. And, the increase in confidence impacts the motivation level. At this point, the employee is ripe for the influences of their individual manager and project team.

The Audition Phase typically lasts thirty days post new hire training.

Phase IV: Aiming Phase
Knowledge: high
Skill: high
Confidence: vulnerable
Motivation: vulnerable

The Aiming Phase is where performance is truly impacted. The Aiming Phase begins when the new employee is handed off to their leader and does not end until the employee leaves the company. It is at this phase that long-term positive performance is molded and company outcomes are achieved. The Aiming Phase is critical to the success of the employee, the leader and the company.

This book is focused on what needs to happen during the Aiming Phase for performance success.

This book, though small in stature, contains those specific strategies to help you become an individual who can influence increased and sustainable performance in others. This book, though few pages, has immense knowledge and tools, that if used correctly, could transcend your leadership abilities and business acumen to a level you never expected out of yourself and others. If the strategies and techniques are followed, you will be able to influence increased performance and impact outcome in your staff, coworkers, family and self.

> *"Ninety-five percent of American managers today say the right thing. Five percent actually do it."*
> *James O'Toole*

Let's take the following pages of this book and unpack the art and science of performance communication. We'll do that by unpacking the following:

- Goals of performance communication
- Pillars of performance communication
- Techniques of performance communication
- Structure of performance communication session

So, what does this mean for you? In a nutshell, it means that you can blend the strategies in this book with your current abilities for immeasurable success in business and relationships. It means you are just a few pages from unlocking potential in others, that otherwise would never be released. It means that you are moments away from becoming a powerful champion of change, influencer of effort and promoter of performance.

Chapter 2

Goals of Performance Communication

Previously we discovered that performance communication is the art and science of using human communication skills and techniques to increase another person's performance. In the recent years employees have gained increasing social influence and greater affluence in the "working world." Because of this, the employee now has more decision-making muscle about where they choose to work and more control over how they choose to spend their time and energy while at work.

The old motivational tools simply don't work with today's employees. Today's employees want to be respected, trusted, given greater authority and greater autonomy. The old "control" style of management simply will not get the performance results from today's employees. I like to say, "Show me an 'unmotivated' employee and I will show you a leader who has not helped that employee achieve his or her full job potential."

No matter the ever shifting and evolving employee environment, improved employee performance is still the goal. Clearly, one of your main goals as a leader in your organization is to increase performance. But, there are a few other goals that are critical to performance communication as well.

Here is the list of all four goals of performance communication:

1) Improve awareness
2) Intensify responsibility
3) Impact behavior change
4) Increase performance

Let's take a look at each of these goals individually.

Improve Awareness

When I think of the concept of awareness, what quickly comes to mind is the sport of basketball, more succinctly, the rule of the pivot foot. In the sport of basketball there is a rule that once you stop dribbling the ball, you must pass the ball or shoot it into the basket. But, there is one more piece to this rule, which is the pivot. Once you stop dribbling, you are allowed to keep one foot planted on the ground and turn, or pivot, on that foot.

What's the point of the pivot? The point is to allow the player the ability to see the whole court and all the potential options of passing the ball.

If you are tracking this analogy, I would imagine you know where I am going. Improving awareness is helping the other person use their pivot foot, helping them see the full picture, where they fit into that picture and all of their options and choices. Improving awareness is giving them the opportunity for a 360 degree perspective. Awareness is knowing what is relevant to the situation, the dynamics of the relationships between the people and the projects in the company.

Think about this—imagine you're in a room that is completely dark. Not a single thread of light is visible. You can't even see your hand in front of your face. Add to this pitch black room some interesting sounds. To your right you hear a scratching sound as if some foreign creature is attempting to get loose. To your left you hear the sound of light taps, reminding you of large spiders crawling on the floor toward you.

What are your thoughts at this very moment? What is your physical state? I would imagine if you are like me, you are about ready to jump out of your skin.

Now, what if you were given a tiny pin light? What if you were given a flash light? What if someone turned on the lights? With each new amount of light, you were given a greater awareness of your surroundings. And, based on this new level of awareness you were able to make different choices and decisions.

Let's close out this dark room scenario by telling you what the sounds were. You look to your right...to your left...only to discover it was just pre-recorded sounds being played over and over. So it's ok to get back into your skin, for those of you who jumped out.

Now that you have this new awareness, what are your thoughts at this very moment? What is your physical state? I would venture to guess they are drastically different than before. What changed? Only your awareness changed. But, based on this awareness there is a greater clarity of perception and a better vantage point from which to make decisions and to take action.

In sum, improving awareness is helping someone pivot for perspective and assisting them in turning on the lights. When it comes to performance communication, improving awareness is imperative.

If, through your communication, you can have as a goal to assist another to become more aware, you offer them some incredible benefits: broader perspective, more information, a greater ability to make decisions, and more choices. As performance coach, John Whitmore, states, "I am able to control only that of which I am aware. That of which I am unaware controls me."

At this point, you are probably drooling for information on just how do you improve awareness. The answer to that will come soon enough. For now, suffice to say improve awareness and you will improve performance.

Intensify Responsibility

Take a look at this short poem attributed to Charles Osgood, titled "Everybody, Anybody, Somebody and Nobody."

There was a most important job that needed to be done,
And no reason not to do it, there was absolutely none.

But in vital matters such as this the thing you have to ask,
Is who exactly will it be who'll carry out this task.

ANYBODY could have told you that EVERYBODY knew,
That this was something SOMEBODY would surely have to do.

NOBODY was unwilling, ANYBODY had the ability,

But NOBODY thought he was supposed to be the one.

It seemed to be a job that ANYBODY could have done,
If ANYBODY thought he was supposed to be the one.

But since EVERYBODY recognized that ANYBODY could,
EVERYBODY took for granted that SOMEBODY would.

But, NOBODY told ANYBODY that we are aware of,
That he would be in charge of seeing it was taken care of.

And NOBODY took it on himself to follow through and do,
What EVERYBODY thought that SOMEBODY would do.

When what EVERYBODY needs did not get done at all,
EVERYBODY was complaining that SOMEBODY dropped the ball.

ANYBODY then could see it was an awful crying shame,
And EVERYBODY looked around for SOMEBODY to blame.

SOMEBODY should have done the job and EVERYBODY would have. But in the end, NOBODY did what ANYBODY could have.

This comical, yet all too true, poem represents the plight of many a leader, manager, sales professional and business owner…lack of responsibility from others.

One of the core goals of performance communication is to intensify responsibility in others. Responsibility is being answerable and accountable for one's own actions, power, efforts and outcomes.

About a year ago, I was sitting in an airport waiting to board a flight to a conference. I noticed that every time I looked up at the flight status it kept getting more and more delayed. Well, as you have probably experienced, a "reasons buzz" quickly started to wave across the awaiting passengers.

In the span of minutes, I heard the flight was delayed due to weather in a different city. They didn't have enough food on board to match the number of passengers, and you know how some people can get when they don't get their tiny bag of three mixed nuts. But, I also overheard that the flight didn't have a flight crew assigned. This rumor made me curious. So I slowly started to make my way toward the gate agents. I got close enough to hear them talking about how the flight crew reserve list was already depleted and that we were all going to have to wait until another flight came in and steal that flight crew.

Well, after about an hour and a half delay, a flight crew was being hurriedly escorted to the plane. At that moment, amongst the sarcastic cheers and clapping of the waiting passengers, I realized this importance of responsibility.

I don't know much about managing flight schedules and crew schedules, but I can imagine it is a logistical nightmare. And, sadly, somewhere along the line, that particular flight fell off the schedule radar. I often wonder if that individual (or individuals) understood the great responsibility that is inherent in their position. I wonder if anyone has ever, in a positive way, expressed to them where their responsibilities fit into the bigger operational purpose.

The second goal of performance communication is to intensify responsibility. When you can intensify responsibility in another person through your communication, you effectively avoid the "pointing or praise phenomena." The "pointing or praise phenomena" is when something incorrect happens, I point out who/what/why it wasn't my fault. When something positive happens, I eagerly express who/what/why I deserve the praise. This phenomenon can quickly kill any growth in a department or company and can slice away at the morale of employees.

"Intensifying responsibility is not telling someone what to do louder and more often."
Corey Pruitt

The methods to appropriately intensify responsibility will be expressed in future chapters. For now, lock in your memory that intensifying responsibility is allowing the other person to truly accept, choose and take ownership over their thoughts and actions. When this occurs, commitment increases. And, when commitment increases, so does performance.

Impact Behavior Change

Recall back to your college freshman year (or "years" for a few of us), when you took Introduction to Psychology. Or that time when you had a wild idea to thumb through that psychology book in the bookstore. You probably hazily recall a few things. One, you remember you read something about making your dog drool by ringing a bell; and you recall there was a lot of information about behaviors.

Although, this book is not going to be your recap of Intro to Psychology, it will provide you with what you need to know about the third goal of performance communication: impact behavior change.

When the ultimate goal is performance improvement, the conversation will, at some point, involve methods and techniques to change behaviors for the long term.

To break it down to the bare-bones, there are really three components one must know in order to truly change behaviors: (1) behaviors, (2) reasons, and (3) beliefs. Let's take a few minutes to ground ourselves in these three components.

I like to think about behavior change as an iceberg. At the top of the iceberg, the part you can see above the water is "behavior." Just below the water's surface is "reason." And deep below the surface is "belief."

Behavior—

Behavior is what we can see. It is the only observable portion of the iceberg. Often, when we think about changing behaviors, we don't take the time to stop and think about what constitutes a behavior, and is it really what we are trying to change?

Behaviors are observable actions or reactions of a person in response to one's perception of what is going on inside and outside of that person.

Take a few examples: I'm hungry (the stimuli), I get off my rear and go the kitchen to get something to eat (the behavior). You're cold (the stimuli), you put on a jacket (the behavior). Your staff feels like they are being singled out or reprimanded (the stimuli); they get defensive and angry (the behavior). I think you get the idea.

So, what do you need to know about this piece of the behavior change iceberg? First, behaviors are the outcome. They are the indicators of what is going on inside and around you and your staff. Second, if you are staying above the water line, then you will not be impacting behavior change for the long term. You must dive deeper to the level of reasons.

Reason—

All behaviors have a motive, a rationale, a meaning behind them. All behaviors have a reason. Reasons are the basis or motive to explain or justify an action or decision.

You have probably heard the story about the mother who was preparing ham one night for dinner. As she was preparing the ham, she cut off both ends and set them aside. Her son asked her why she did that, and she responded, "It's what grandma does, I'm not sure why." The next day the mother was talking with Grandma, "Why do you cut the ends off the ham?" She replied, "That is what my mother always did." That night, they went to the Great Grandmother's house and asked her the same question, "Why do we all cut the ends off the ham before we cook it?" The Great Grandmother replied, "I don't know why you all do it, I just never had a pan big enough to cook an entire ham."

You see, all behaviors serve a purpose. Even if the purpose seems "crazy" or "insignificant" it is a good enough reason for the behavior to result.

Two of my boys were wrestling one day, when all of the sudden, one reared back and slugged the other right in the gut. When asked why he punched his brother, he replied, "Because he was going to punch me." What's the lesson here? Not only do people behave because of what is actually happening, people also behave because of what they perceive is going to happen.

So, what do you need to know about this piece of the behavior change iceberg? First, all behaviors serve a purpose. Humans are not random beings. Our behaviors have a reason behind them. Second, reasons can be based on reality and on perception of what *may* happen. Third, if you are just floating around the reasons level of the iceberg, then you will not be impacting behavior change for the long term. You must dive deeper to the level of belief.

Belief -

The belief level is where true change happens. It is not until someone's beliefs have been altered that their reasons shift and their behaviors follow.

The beliefs level is so important for many reasons. Chief among them is this: people's motivation, emotions, actions and performances are based more on what they believe than on what is objectively true. Put simply, beliefs will be—and are—the ultimate impact factor of behavior. What we believe about an event, situation or person will, in the end, determine how we act and react to that event, situation or person.

Let's quickly unpack four questions: What are beliefs? How are they formed? Why are they so powerful? What does this have to do with performance communication?

What are beliefs? Beliefs are *generalizations*, rooted in *emotions*, and backed by perception and a feeling of *certainty*. There are some key words here that really give us some good insight into what beliefs really are.

The first is generalizations. Beliefs are a collection of generalizations that have been supported over time. Take for example, generalizations you have about people. Fill in the blanks, "Republicans are _____." "Democrats are _____." "CEO's are _____." "Managers are _____." I bet you were able to quickly fill in the blanks. What you inserted were your beliefs. What you inserted were generalizations. Generalizations are not necessarily bad, as they help us function in society and business. They help us learn, make decisions and store information.

The second buzz word regarding beliefs is emotions. Beliefs are rooted in emotion. That is what makes them so powerful; so passion filled. Many motives and intentions are entrenched in emotion.

Certainty: Beliefs are backed by a perception and feeling of certainty. Certainty is the level of emotional intensity that is attached. Look at the level of certainty progress in the following words: idea, opinion, belief, conviction. Clearly, you can grasp the increase of certainty within the string of words.

Again, beliefs are *generalizations*, rooted in *emotions*, and backed by perception and a feeling of *certainty*.

How are beliefs formed? Beliefs are like a rope. Let me explain. Rope is formed by taking strands of spun fibers and twisting them together. The individual strands are not as strong by themselves, but twisted with other strands become strong enough to pull a boat, cars, suspend bridges, climb mountains, etc. Beliefs are like ropes; they are made up of individual strands, and over time, are multiplied, enforced and reinforced to form a belief that is as strong as a rope.

There are five primary belief strands that form ones belief rope: personal experiences, vicarious experiences, information, thoughts and interpretations. These five strands, when continuously reinforced will form a solid rope, a belief.

Think of how your past experiences often influence your current decisions and experiences. Think of how the experiences of others color your choices. Or, how information can add to re-inforce what you believe or know.

Why are beliefs so powerful? Beliefs are powerful because they allow us to more quickly make decisions and make sense out of our reality. Beliefs are powerful because they are continually strengthened by strong influences. Beliefs are powerful because they quickly guide our thoughts and actions away from perceived pain and toward perceived pleasure. Beliefs are powerful because they determine the quality of our performance.

What do beliefs have to do with performance communication? In short, everything. You can only lead people to change their own beliefs. You cannot change someone else's beliefs for them. The goal is to pace and lead them into creating a new belief for themselves.

Now that you know the behavior change iceberg, you know that beliefs impact reasons and reasons impact behaviors. If your ultimate goal is to increase the performance of others, you must understand that humans are more driven by what they believe, than by reality. Albert Bandura, renowned psychologist, said "what people think, believe and feel affects how they behave." If I were to alter this quote to fit this book, it would read, "What people believe is how they perform."

Increase Performance

The fourth and final goal of performance communication is to increase performance. The irony of this goal is, if you have improved awareness, intensified responsibility and impacted behavior change, then the result will be increased performance.

So there you have it, four goals of performance communication. Now the million dollar question, "how do you reach these goals?" Let's start by looking at the principles of performance communication.

Chapter 3

Principles of Performance Communication

There are three things in life that are difficult to do: build a pyramid from the top down; eat a bagel from the inside out; and be successful with performance communication without knowing the principles.

There are five principles to get you grounded in the art and science of performance communication
- Listening
- Open questions
- Offer options
- Preferences language
- Support self-efficacy

These five principles form the foundation upon which the techniques and structure of performance communication are built. To truly influence increased performance, you must know and apply these principles.

Listening

Listening is one of the most important, and most underused, communication skills. How well you listen will have a major impact on all your relationships—both personal and professional. How well you listen will have a major impact on your effectiveness in increasing performance in others.

By becoming an effective listener you will:
- Improve productivity
- Improve your ability to influence
- Improve your ability to negotiate
- Lessen conflict and misunderstandings
- Increase the confidence of others
- Gain cooperation from others
- Gain trust and credibility
- Obtain more accurate and valid information
- Amplify professional success
- Increase performance in others

That is quite the laundry list of positive benefits to being an effective listener. Clearly listening is a skill to integrate into your daily management practice.

Here are four actions to take to ensure you are an effective listener.

1) Seek understanding. One of your primary goals for listening should be to seek understanding. That is, to seek understanding of the other persons perspective. Your personal filters, assumptions, judgments and beliefs can easily distort what you hear. As an effective listener, your role is to understand what is being said.

In any communication situation there are two messages: the message being expressed and the message being heard. Often, they are two different messages.

A teacher was practicing addition with her class when she asked her student the following question:

Teacher: "If I give you two rabbits, two rabbits, and another two rabbits, how many rabbits do you have?"

Sally: "Seven!"

Teacher: "No. Listen carefully. If I give you two rabbits, two rabbits, and another two rabbits, how many rabbits do you have?"

Sally: "Seven!"

Teacher: "Let's try this another way. If I give you two apples, two apples, and two apples, how many apples do you have?"

Sally: "Six!"

Teacher: "Good, now, if I give you two rabbits, two rabbits, and another two rabbits, how many rabbits do you have?"

Sally: "Seven!"

Teacher: "Sally, how on earth do you work out three lots of two rabbits equals seven?"

Sally: "I've already got one rabbit at home now."

Although comical, the teacher did not seek little Sally's understanding until after asking the same question three times and expecting a different answer. Sadly, this is not a far stretch from the business world. The questions may be more elaborate, but the approach is the same…asking the same question over and over and not listening in order to seek understanding.

Effective listeners truly seek understanding from others. There are three key benefits of seeking understanding: if the other person feels understood, usually they will talk more; the other person will view you as a good communicator; you have a better perspective to tailor your communication to the other person.

2)   Focus. Effective listeners focus. That is, concentrating your efforts and attention on one thing…the other person. In today's business culture of quantum-tasking (that's multitasking on steroids), information drowning, and strategic resource allocation (fancy talk for giving more work to less people), it's difficult to focus.

At the same time, increasing performance in others hinges upon your ability to focus on what is being said. It hinges upon your ability to listen for key ideas, withhold judgments, listen critically, and eliminate listening obstacles.

Effective listeners maintain focus when communicating with others.

3)   Respond to what is being said. One of my sons would fall into the category of listener I call the non-responders. I can be explaining something that is so exciting and he won't move a muscle to show he is listening. Now, this skill of his comes in great when he is playing poker, but not so hot when communicating with others in everyday life.

You can wrap this element of effective listening into one word, acknowledgement. Acknowledge, by responding to what is being said. That is, display you're listening by providing some type of verbal and nonverbal feedback.

One great technique for responding is to paraphrase or reflect what you just heard. This serves not only to show you are listening, but also to clarify and reinforce the message being received.

Another element to this action of effective listening is the second portion of the sentence, "Respond to what is being said." So often you get caught up in wanting more information from someone, so you can put out the fire, that you totally bypass what they just said and you insert your own agenda. There is a time for that, be sure you respond to what they said first.

Effective listeners consistently respond to what is being said.

4)   Summarize. This is your last line of defense against miscommunication. Summarizing captures the main points of the conversation and nicely, and succinctly, expresses them once more. Summarizing also allows the other person one last time to ensure you did not miss anything important about what they said. Effective listeners always summarize.

Whether it be relational or professional, effective listening is imperative for successful performance communication. Effective listening is a dynamic method of listening that consists of seeking understanding, focused attention, responding to what is being said, and summarizing.

Seven Listening Traps

When discovering how to be a more effective listener, you must also glimpse into the listening traps. Everyone visits these listening traps from time to time. The goal is to become more aware of your listening so you can avoid these traps at all costs.

1. Assumer: Assuming you know what the speaker is trying to say, or is going to say.

2. Advisor: You attempt to problem solve without hearing the feelings and acknowledging the speaker.

3. Battler: You interrupt, argue or debate. Your only goal for listening is to catch inaccuracies so you can show your own knowledge on the subject at hand.

4. Identifier: Everything an individual tells you, you refer back to your own experiences. Sometimes, you will launch a story before they can finish theirs. Your main listening goal is to respond or start talking again.

5. Rehearser: Your attention is focused on what you are going to say next, not on what the other person is saying.

6. Non-responder: Stagnant listener. You give no feedback at all to show you are listening.

7. Splitter: You listen to some things and not others. Your mind wanders during the conversation. Pre-occupied with something else. You are only half listening and a trigger sets off a chain of private associations.

Be aware of your primary listening traps and begin to make it a habit to employ effective listening with your staff.

Open Questions

Open questions are a powerful principle. Open questions are questions that invite elaboration. Open question cannot be answered with a simple "yes" or "no" response.

Open questions are not only a powerful principle for increasing performance; they are a powerful tool as well. They are powerful because:

- They provide the opportunity for the other person to think and process.
- They invite the other person to express themselves more fully.
- They encourage the other person to do more of the talking.
- They develop a dialogue and conversation.
- They elicit details.
- They uncover the other persons' opinions, knowledge, feelings, thoughts and issues.

For all these reasons, open questions will be your primary principle for creating conversation—exchanging information—to increase performance.

The fundamental concept which makes open questions so potent for increasing performance is this: the more people talk, the more they become aware of what they believe and the more you come to understand their perspective. Whatever the content, central to performance communication is, people do not want to be told what to do; nor do they want someone else's answers. Instead, they want help finding their own.

It was halftime. I was surrounded by a bunch of 11 year old sweaty boys. The entire first half I was doing my best coaching. I was shouting plays, barking about defense and yelling about passing the ball and moving around the court. I kneeled down and looked up at the young, red, faces and said, "boys, we are down by 15 points, what do you want to do to close the gap?"

Then I closed my mouth. One boy raised his hand and said, "coach, I guess I could pass more!" Another boy said, "I could move without the ball and help others get open, too!" I replied, "Great, boys! How about on defense, what do you think will make the biggest difference?" They proceeded to tell me all the ways to close the point gap. It was all the same stuff I had been telling them to do the entire first half.

The second half of the game, they closed the 15 point gap and even took the lead for a few minutes. The team ended up losing the game, but I reinforced a lesson in myself. The first half I was not communicating effectively; I was not using the power of open ended questions.

When I changed my approach, I got more than just ideas from the boys, I got buy in...I got responsibility, as it was now their idea and they were going to put forth effort to prove their ideas would work.

"The person who asks the right questions, learns the most."
John Maxwell

We will go into more details when you get to techniques of performance communication as well as structuring your performance communication sessions.

Offer Options

You have probably heard the story about the pastor who was visiting the house of one of his older members. There was a bowl of peanuts on the coffee table that he snacked on as they visited. When it was time to leave, he graciously thanked the elderly lady for her time and hospitality. He especially thanked her for the peanuts. She said, "Oh, you're welcome. Ever since I lost my dentures, all I can do is suck the chocolate off of them."

At that moment I bet the pastor wished he had other options than just peanuts on the coffee table.

The third principle of performance communication is offer options. Options and choices are what allow another person to feel a part of the communication and decision making process. Options are what allow another person to intensify responsibility and improve awareness.

Here are four strong reasons to offer options whenever possible:

1) Options build rapport. Part of performance communication is relationship building.

2) Options create an open and supportive communication environment, which in turn, increases the likelihood of improved performance from others.

3) Options allow others to consider various ideas, suggestions, thoughts and behaviors. This inherently creates a sense of responsibility and ownership of the eventual behaviors and outcomes.

4) Options soften the information and feedback sharing process. Instead of just "telling" someone what to do, providing them options creates collaboration and responsibility.

Offering options is a solid principle when your goal is increased performance in others. So, make it your aim to actively foster other's perception of choice through your communication. Make it your aim to avoid directing, giving orders or imperatives. Make it your aim to express you respect the other persons' choices, control and perspective.

This particular principle will really come into play when you structure your performance communication sessions, which will unfold in an upcoming chapter.

Preference Language

While I was doing some consulting, and conducting training for a small group of managers and a few frontline staff, I recall one woman who continually repeated what I was saying. But, she would not say the exact same thing. She would change some of the words, but clearly the concepts and ideas were still the same. This went on for a while, and quite frankly, got really old really quick.

During one of the breaks I approached the woman to ask how she was enjoying the information. She replied that she was finding the information very helpful. She then went on to tell me all the ways I "should" have been explaining the information.

It took everything in my power not to share with her the hundreds of thoughts that where filling my mind. I, trying to be the hired professional, politely thanked her for her comments and quickly retreated to the whiteboard and pretended to ponder what to write. In reality, I was pondering what had just happened.

She had told me she was finding the information helpful and enjoyable, but had to change everything I was saying. It was then that this principle struck me. I was not communicating in the language style and preference that suited her. When she was repeating me, she was actually translating what I was saying in my language preference to her language preference.

The fourth principle of performance communication is "preference language." Excellent performance communicators pick up on the language preferences of others. Not only do they pick up on it, but they adjust their language accordingly.

Preference language is the communication system that is most preferred by another. Adjectives, verbs and adverbs make up the predicates used in speech, and offer insight into the person's preferred communication system.

Proponents of Neurolinguistic Programming (NLP) tell us for each person, one sense is stronger than the other. People use all three of the main systems in their speech—visual, auditory and kinesthetic—although everyone prefers one over the other.

So, for you visual folks, "let's take a look at these three language preferences." For you auditory folks, "let's ensure these concepts click by exploring them more." And for you kinesthetic folks, "let's break down these concepts."

Visual Preference

Visual people "see" their world. They use words like "focus," "clear," "foggy," "hazy." They "get the picture" or "see the bottom line." Visual people often provide you clues of their preference with their nonverbal communication also. Visual people tend to look up when they speak as a way of accessing their visual channels, where such information is neurologically housed.

For example, when you ask a visual preference person to describe something for you, they are inclined to construct the memory by looking up.

What should you do with the information about people with a visual preference for language? When communicating with visual people, use visual empathizers to make them think you see the world the way they do.

For example, "After looking over that business proposal, what are some things that caught your eye?" And, "Now that you know the magnitude of this project and our aggressive timeline, what do you see being your first action?"

Auditory Preference

Auditory people hear their world. Things are "out of harmony" or "things just click." Auditory preference people will "hear what you're saying," and will often say, "I hear ya!" or "Hear you loud and clear!" Auditory people tend to move their eyes left to right as a way of accessing their auditory channels. When the auditory person is constructing or remembering a sound, his eyes will move from one side to the other.

How are you to communicate with auditory people to improve your ability to improve performance in others? Use auditory empathizers to make them think you hear them loud and clear.

For example, "After reading through the business proposal how does it sound to you?" And, "Now that you know the magnitude of this project and our aggressive timeline, what sounds like a logical first action for you?"

Kinesthetic Preference

The last of the three main systems is kinesthetic. Kinesthetic people feel their world. They "sense" something is wrong. They can "feel" the tension in the room. They think you are being "pushy." They feel like they are "carrying the load" Nonverbally, kinesthetic preference people tend to look down and toward their dominant hand when accessing memories.

To best communicate with the individual that prefers kinesthetic language, use kinesthetic empathizers to make them think you feel the same way they do.

For example, "Now that you have walked through the business proposal, what are some things that jumped out at you?" And, "Now that you know the magnitude of this project and our aggressive timeline, what will your first steps be?"

Bottom line: Be a performance communication strategist. Listen to your staff's every word for clues to his or her preference language. The evidence is spewing from their lips. Then, act on that communication preference and tailor your performance communication to that individual.

Support Self-Efficacy

Tyrone "Muggsy" Bogues, Earl Boykins, Anthony "spud" Webb. What do all three of these men have in common? They all were extremely successful in the sport of basketball.

So, what's the big deal? The big deal is that the average height in the NBA is 6 feet 7 inches. Bogues, Boykins and Webb are 5 foot 3 inches, 5 foot 5 inches and 5 foot 7 inches respectively. In a sport that is dominated by physical size, some athletes as big as 7 foot 4 inches, these men excelled.

Muggsy Bogues played 14 years in the NBA and was a regular among NBA leaders in assists and steals. Spud Webb was the 1986 Slam-dunk Champion, and defeated many high-flying athletes who were more than a foot taller than he was. Earl Boykins was an All-American in college and finished 2nd in the nation for scoring. In the NBA he holds the record for most points scored in overtime. Clearly, all three players have made an impact on the game of basketball in spite of their smaller size.

So, why the basketball lesson? Because each of these men possessed something that pushed them to excel in an environment that consistently told them "no," in an athletic culture that continually catered to taller and larger men. That "something" is called self-efficacy.

The last principle of performance communication is supporting self-efficacy. Self-efficacy is one's belief in themselves, that they have the ability to be successful at a particular task or endeavor. In short, self-efficacy is the answer to the question that everyone asks, "can I do this?"

Self-efficacy was first described by a Stanford University Psychology Professor, Albert Bandura, in the 1970's and has gained scientific support and notoriety over the years.

When it comes to performance communication, self-efficacy is critical as it provides the foundation for human motivation. That is, people's motivation, actions, and performance are based more on what they believe than on what is objectively true. For this reason, how people behave and perform can often be better predicted by the beliefs they hold about their abilities than by what they are actually capable of accomplishing.

Bogues, Boykins and Webb all had a high sense of self-efficacy which propelled them to perform in spite of the environment and circumstances of physical height. Self-efficacy beliefs provide a motivation so that your actual behavior can begin to develop and rise. The great thing about self-efficacy beliefs is that they are not intended to always match existing reality.

Self-efficacy beliefs contribute to motivation and performance in several ways: they determine the choices we make, how much effort we expend, and how long we persevere.

Self-efficacy beliefs influence the choices people make. The choices people make and the courses of action they pursue are influenced by what they believe about personal abilities. Most people, you and I included, tend to select tasks and activities in which they feel competent and confident, and avoid those in which they do not.

Career choice, health choices, extracurricular activities, goals and job duties are all choices people filter through their self-efficacy beliefs. There are countless attractive options people don't pursue because they lack the belief in their capabilities. It is by the choices they make, people cultivate different competencies, interests, social networks, and professional skills that determine life courses.

I will be the first to tell you, I am not a golfer. I will also be the first to tell you I wish I was a golfer. I can wish all day that I am good at golf, but wishing won't influence my performance. It's not until my self-efficacy belief is enhanced that I will choose to play golf over other sports.

Self-efficacy beliefs influence the effort people will expend on an activity. If an individual perceives there is no hope or possibility of success, then no effort will be made. Individuals with an assurance in their capabilities approach tasks as worthy of their efforts and will expend the effort to be successful.

Self-efficacy beliefs influence how long one will persevere when confronting obstacles. Perseverance is directly related to one's belief in their ability to succeed. Unless people believe that their actions can produce the outcomes they desire, they have little incentive to act or persevere in the face of difficulties.

Those who have a strong belief in their capabilities assert greater effort when they feel they may be failing to master the challenge. And, of course, strong perseverance contributes to performance accomplishments.

If self-efficacy beliefs influence one's choices, efforts and perseverance, how can you support someone's self-efficacy?

There are three primary sources for supporting self-efficacy:
- Mastery experience
- Vicarious experience
- Social persuasion

Let's quickly unpack each of these and see how they fit into performance communication.

One avenue for supporting self-efficacy is through personal mastery experience. When someone experiences personal success in a particular area, that success creates a strong self-belief of efficacy. On the same token, failure undermines one's self-efficacy belief. There is more to accomplishing something or performing a certain way than just knowing how to. That "something" is personal mastery experience.

So, how do you build mastery experiences in others? Create opportunities for success and allow the individual to walk through that success. It has been said that success creates success. Structure situations for people in ways that bring success (even in small doses) and avoid placing them in situations prematurely where they are likely to fail often.

The second avenue for supporting self-efficacy is through vicarious experiences. Seeing another person similar to oneself succeed by sustained effort increases the observer's beliefs that they, too, possess the capabilities to master comparable activities required to succeed.

The final avenue for supporting self-efficacy is through social persuasion. In short, people who are persuaded verbally that they possess the capabilities to master given activities are more likely to mobilize greater effort and sustain that effort. To that end, the extent that these verbal boosts increase perceived self-efficacy lead people to try hard enough to succeed; they also promote development of skills which lead to a sense of self-efficacy.

To simplify this, put people in incremental situations to be successful...put them around others who are already successful at the task...and encourage them that you know they can be successful. Then you will support another's self-efficacy.

Chapter 4

Techniques of Performance Communication

The business plan had been drafted. The financial projections had been nicely inserted into a spreadsheet. I had even ordered the business cards. I was getting ready to start my first business. It was time to share my great business idea with my wife. I wanted to remind her just how great a guy she married.

She looked over the plan and projections. Commented on how professional it all appeared. Then she looked me right in the eyes, and with a beautiful smile on her face, she said, "what do you do next?"

What do I do next? That is not what I wanted to hear! I was wanting a, "oh honey, you are so smart! What a great idea! This business will surely work out! I knew I married a smart and successful man!" And, all I got was a, "what do you do next?"

After a few moments of shock, I came to my senses and realized what my wife was saying. She was really saying, "Honey, you have come up with great ideas before, have completed the same process, have been all excited, have made the family all excited only for the idea to fade into a filing cabinet of ideas. What action are you going to take to make this one work?"

Action! Performance communication is only effective when the desired action results from the interaction. Performance is all about sustained action. The following six techniques will assist you in creating communication which leads to sustained effective performance and communication which leads to action.

1) Assess motivation
2) Connect to DNA
3) Transformation talk, DNA
4) Initiate an action plan
5) Offer affirmations and empathy
6) Negotiate resistance

In the next few pages you will focus on each of these six techniques to unpack their merit, use and effectiveness in performance communication.

Assess Motivation

Rick was diagnosed as spastic quadriplegic with cerebral palsy, and is confined to an electronic wheel chair. In the spring of 1977, Rick told his father he wanted to participate in a charity run for someone who was recently paralyzed in an accident. Rick's father, far from being a distance runner, agreed to push Rick in his wheelchair throughout the five mile race. They finished the race, and that night Rick told his father, "Dad, when I'm running it feels like I'm not handicapped" (www.teamhoyt.com).

Rick and his father, Dick Hoyt, have since competed in over 1000 races, including marathons, triathlons and Ironman competitions. And, in 1992, this father and son team biked across the U.S. in just 45 days.

From parents like Dick Hoyt, who exhibit superhuman strength and stamina for their children to employees who exhibit incredible performance potential. From athletes that rise after defeat to executives that emerge in spite of circumstances. From single mothers who do whatever is necessary to support their families to the Olympian who strives for nothing less than gold. What do they all have in common? What do they all share? They are all displaying motivation.

If the end result is for action to stem from your interaction you must ground yourself in motivation and assessing motivation in others.

What is motivation? Motivation is anything which instigates one to engage in a particular behavior to satisfy a specific internal state. Let's break this definition down to its main aspects.

- Instigates one to engage in a behavior. To instigate is to put into action, to cause, to provoke. Motivation is anything that causes a particular action or a particular behavior.
- Satisfy a specific internal state. The term internal state is a fancy way of saying, "need, want, desire, or goals." Of course, this internal state is impacted by what's going on externally. Nevertheless, the internal state is what energizes and directs the ultimate behavior. We will talk more about this internal state idea later.

Motivation is occurring all the time. In fact, the very word "motivation" stems from the Latin word for "movement." There are constant influences which instigate one to move, to engage, in a particular behavior.

Everything an individual does, whether intentional or seemingly unintentional, positive or negative, is the result of motivation. Now, you may be saying, "what about the staff member I have who does the minimal work necessary. Who seems fine with getting "average" reviews. Is this staff member "motivated?"

In one emphatic word, "yes!" This staff member is engaged in a particular behavior (just enough to get by) to satisfy an internal state (possibly, I need a job, so I will do what is necessary to keep my job...or...once they start paying me what I am worth, then I will show them what kind of job I am really capable of producing). This staff member is not lacking motivation; she is merely more motivated to remain in her current state than to put forth the effort to change.

Typically, we think of motivation as being the driving force toward something we want. It is also the driving force keeping us right where we are.

The driving force of motivation can either be external or internal. Both come into play when you are trying to reach goals, impact another's performance and increase or decrease a particular behavior.

External Motivation

I was consulting for a large medical company a few years back. They were having an issue with the medical staff not truly focusing on the patient. Instead, they were focusing on their documentation and performance measures. I was brought in to help figure out how to motivate the medical staff to still meet the documentation and performance standards while putting the focus on the needs of the patient.

I started my analysis with an easy question, "what have you already tried?" The answer to this question gave a huge clue to the solution. The upper management replied, "We have tried everything. We have given out awards, we have attached financial increases to certain patient-centered behaviors, we have had huge recognition ceremonies, we have even had trainers come in and speak about customer service...we have tried everything."

What did they really tell me, as they answered my question? They told me they tried many ways of motivating, all of which were external. Rewards, incentives, bonuses—all are forms of external motivators.

External motivating factors compel people to do something or act in a certain way because of factors external to him or her. There is a basic psychological truth: people will continue to do what is getting noticed. Put that in the business world and it would sound like this, "you get what is rewarded."

Extensive research supports that human behavior is shaped by consequences, and one powerful way to enhance employee performance is by providing positive consequences for performance. If you recognize and reward a specific behavior, that behavior will tend to be repeated.

Budgets are tight, raises and promotions are locked, layoffs are epidemic. In today's economic times, company resources are at an all-time low. Here is a quick list of fruitful external motivators that won't break the company bank:

- Recognition
- Chance to develop new skills
- Involvement in making some decisions
- Provide opportunities to meet new people
- Show appreciation of work done

The External Motivation Issue

I often diagnose companies and leaders with "super-cloud syndrome." Super markets use loyalty points and discounts to spur a behavior. Airlines use air or "cloud" mile programs to instigate a continued behavior. The super-cloud syndrome is simply, staying with external motivators when internal would prove more effective.

The problem with the external motivators, the "super-cloud syndrome" is when the rewards stop, the behaviors often stop also. External motivators may be successful in the short term, but their sustainability is always wavering. The main reason for the short lived motivation is that the "super-cloud syndrome" focuses people on the reward not the action. Stop the reward and the action stops too.

So, what was my first recommendation for this medical company? My first recommendation was to change the motivating factors from completely external to internal. Stephen Covey notes, "Motivation is fire from within. If someone else tries to light that fire under you, chances are it will burn very briefly."

Internal Motivation

Often you have to start with external motivators until you figure out the internal. Internal motivation occurs when people are motivated to do something because it brings them pleasure, they think it is important, or they feel that how they are behaving is significant.

Let's revisit the medical company. Our internal motivation strategy had one primary action. First, we had a large conference with all the front line medical staff that were interfacing with the patients. At this conference we initiated a large conversation that went something like this:

Consultant: "Our main purpose today is to find out from your perspective, in which areas you would like to develop professionally. We are going to get at it a little differently than usual. But, before we get too far into the conversation, I would love to hear from some of you as to why you started to practice medicine?"

Audience: "…to help people…" "…to assist others in being healthier…" "…to save lives…" "…change bad habits…"

Consultant: "It sounds like the overarching theme is a strong desire to help people live healthier and more satisfying lives. Very admirable! What are a few things you are currently doing that are helping you grow professionally and at the same time meeting the need of helping others live healthier and more satisfying lives?"

Audience: "I'm up to date on the latest medical knowledge and treatment options." "I maintain my certifications and licenses...."

Consultant: "Excellent, ensuring you're sound in the latest treatments, preventions, etc. and maintaining licensure is imperative for your success. If you will allow me, I would like to dive deeper. Help me make the connection from you having knowledge that is up to date to helping others have better health."

Audience: "...we are able to make better assessments and give better advice..." "...we are able to give people more options..."

Consultant: "Let's take a short step back and summarize where we are right now. You have told me that the reason you got into medicine was to help others be healthier. Currently, you maintain a sound and current knowledge base of medicine, treatment, prevention, etc. Also, you use this knowledge to better assess the patients you work with and provide them better advice and recommendations. So, what happens when you have great knowledge, give great information and advice, and the patient does not act on it? How are you satisfying that original need of helping others live healthier lives?"

Audience: Silence...cricket chirp...cricket chirp...

Consultant: "It sounds like you all really want to develop professionally in your ability to improve your communication skills to increase patient compliance with practitioner's orders. Does that sound like an avenue that will help satisfy your desire to help others live healthier lives?"

The conversation continued with collectively creating a schedule of training events and brainstorming ideas. But, what was really happening throughout the conversation was leading the audience to perform differently by anchoring their actions to internal motivating factors. That was, their desire to be significant by helping others lead healthier lives.

It is becoming increasingly difficult to keep employees motivated and committed to the company's mission. Motivated employees make all the difference in the rapidly changing workplace that today's economy demands. Just remember, the more internally motivated an individual is, the better the outcome.

> *"Motivation is the art of getting people to do what you want them to do because they want to do it."*
> *Dwight D. Eisenhower*

Zoom out with me for a moment. Your first performance communication action is to assess motivation. So far, you have defined motivation and reviewed external and internal motivation. Now, shift focus onto the three elements of assessing motivation.

Ready, willing and able. These three factors are what influence a person's behaviors and performance. You see, people will not sustain a particular performance because someone tells them they "need" to. People will sustain a performance behavior because they:

- Believe that it is important from their perspective,
- are willing to put forth the effort necessary to be successful because they believe the behavior will be worth it, and

-        are confident they can be successful and that the behavior will lead to the desired result.

Jim is married with four kids. He talked incessantly about breaking out of the nine-to-five and starting his own company. But, it was only talk. What held Jim back from performing to reach his goals?

Was he ready? Jim believed his actions were important. He believed he needed to make the change for his family's future. Jim thought now was the time for him to jump on his business idea.

Was he willing? He believed the necessary effort to be successful would be worth it in the end, and his values supported the effort.

Was he confident in his ability? Jim was unsure in his ability to be successful and was very leery of leaving the comfort of his current position and the stability of income for something not as certain. On a scale of 0—10, Jim was a five.

Ready, willing and able. Three factors which assist in determining the potential for performance behaviors...for motivation. If one of these factors is lacking, the chances for sustained action dramatically decreases. On the other hand, if your assessment reveals one element is lacking, then you know where to focus your efforts for improved performance.

Quick Review
- Ready:
    o The actions must be important from the other person's perspective
    o They must believe there is a need for the action
    o They must feel like now is the time. Limited and/or manageable competing priorities
- Willing
    o They think the actions and effort will be worth it
    o Their values support it
- Able
    o They are confident they can be successful
    o They are confident the behaviors will lead to the desired outcome
    o They have a good plan and support

Whether it's running a marathon or an organization, motivation is always something which instigates one to engage in a particular behavior...motivation always has external and internal elements...and, motivation is always influenced by readiness, willingness and ability.

Chapter 5

Connect to DNA

The second technique which will lead to sustained, effective performance is to connect all behavioral / performance requests to the other person's DNA.

DNA stands for:

- Desire: (wants, longing, yearning, wish)
- Need: (necessity, essential, requirement)
- Aim: (purpose, goal, intention, reason)

Connecting to the person's DNA is essentially answering the question, "Why." If you have ever had kids, know a kid, or have seen a kid, then you know kids like to ask one primary question: "Why?" Kids have a yearning to know the "why" before they know the "how." And, as much as we don't like to admit it, adults are the same way. I always say, adults are just older kids. Adults want to know "why" we are doing everything. We may not ask the question out loud, but we are asking it.

There is a catch to answering this innate question. If your end result is sustained action from your interaction, then just telling someone *your* reasons why they should behave or perform in a certain way will not do the trick.

Quickly revisit some information from earlier in the book:

1) All behaviors have a reason behind them
2) People are motivated to satisfy an internal state
3) People will sustain performance when they are internally motivated

So, you are not just answering the question "why" from your perspective. You are connecting the answer to "why" to the persons DNA (desires, needs, aims).

Take a look at this conversation snippet and how the manager connects the performance to the internal desire, need and aim of the staff member.

"...Todd, this project is much larger in scope than our typical projects. I know you are able to coordinate the logistics. I also know that you desire to be on time with your completion dates and pride yourself in being at or under budget. What are some things you are already thinking of to ensure this project turns out the same way?"

Notice the connection of desired outcomes with factors that are important to the employee. Often, you can easily connect performance with one of the following internal factors:

- Greater autonomy
- Less stress
- Reduced workload
- Increased visibility
- Personal interests
- Reputation
- Impact on co-workers

- Impact on subordinates
- Display of knowledge
- Display of skill / ability

This is just a short list to get your mental juices flowing. Whatever the connection, ensure the behaviors and results are communicated in terms of connection with the staff's DNA (desires, needs, aims).

Bottom line: give your employees a reason that is associated to their DNA and they will produce sustainable results.

Chapter 6

Transformation Talk—DNA

I am no scientist, but one thing I know about biology is, everyone has a unique DNA. My source for this knowledge may be the numerous crime shows I see on TV, nevertheless, the uniqueness of an individuals' DNA cannot be disputed.

When it comes to performance and motivation, everyone has a unique DNA also. However, DNA in this instance stands for desire, need and aim. The previous technique, "connect to DNA," is really only achievable once the staff member has expressed his or her unique DNA.

Let's answer the following three questions:
1)   What is DNA?
2)   How do I come to know my staff's DNA?
3)   What do I do when I know someone's DNA?

Before you explore these three questions, take a look at some of the benefits of extracting DNA:
-   Helps you acquire more information about your staff
-   Makes you appear more conversationally appealing
-   Helps you identify what motivates others
-   Helps build rapport
-   Makes you more influential
-   Allows you to have a stronger ability to lead others in accomplishing a goal or task

What is Transformation Talk—DNA?

Transformation talk is based on a psychological theory called, "Self-perception Theory." This theory expresses when people verbalize their thoughts about their level of ability or reasons to perform a particular behavior; it strengthens the likelihood they will engage in that behavior.

In short, transformation talk is any statement your staff expresses which conveys movement toward a desired action or outcome. It is literally your staff talking themselves into increased performance. The goal of transformation talk is to build intrinsic motivation.

Transformation talk is the individuals "why" behind the actions. Rick Pitino, famed college basketball coach, expresses, "today, people must understand why they're working hard. Every individual in an organization is motivated by something."

Transformation talk usually comes in the form of desire, needs and aim language. For your purposes, it will be beneficial for you to recognize these three indicators within your conversations with others so you can more appropriately gauge the motivation levels of your staff.

Desire: (want, longing, yearning, wish). Statements of desire indicate a wanting or willing toward an action or outcome.

Here is an example of desire language: "I would like to start leaving the office at a decent hour." "I wish I could connect with Jim sooner for this project."

Need: (necessity, essential, requirement). Statements of need indicate a necessity for an action or outcome.

Here is an example of need language: "I absolutely have to get this report done." "I have to get my staff to increase their talk time with our customers."

Aim: (purpose, goal, intention, reason). Statements of aim indicate a reason or purpose for an action or outcome.

Here is an example of aim language: "I will be able to focus on other projects when this is complete." "I have to get this project done because I am going on vacation next month."

How Do I Come To Know My Staff's DNA?

It's one thing to recognize one's DNA, but how do you get your staff to talk this way? How do you come to know your staffs DNA?

Here are four quick ways to get people to talk their DNA?

1) Ask. Through the use of questions you can quickly get answers that are often transformation talk. Here are some examples of questions that evoke transformation talk.
    a. Desire: "What do you want to do about this?" "What are you hoping is the outcome if you follow through with this idea?"

b.   Need: "What do you feel is needed in order for you to be successful with this?" "What are you willing to do about this?"

c.   Aim: "By going this route, what's your goal?" "If you follow through, what would be a few reasons that will push you through the obstacles?"

2)   Explore the pros and cons. This is often a great way to get someone thinking about both sides of the coin and quickly stems to conversations about potential outcomes of performance decisions. To explore, simply ask for the good and bad regarding an action, decision or idea.

3)   Use the double "E's." The double E's are: elaboration and examples. When someone expresses a thought, shares an idea or talks through a project, ask them for more, ask them to clarify certain points, ask for examples.

Here are a few ways to tactfully use the double E's: "Tell me more about..." "In what ways..." "Share an example of..."

4)   Futurecast. Ask what happens if things continue as they are with the issue. Ask what would happen if this or that action shifted. What would the foreseeable action and outcome be?

Of course, there are many ways to get people talking about their desires, needs, and aim. The bottom line is, get people to talk about their DNA and you will come to know their intrinsic motivating factors.

What Do I Do When I Know Someone's DNA?

You may know what transformation talk is, you may know how to get it, but what do you do when you hear it come out of someone's mouth? To answer that question, use the READ acronym:

R: Reflect it. Reflecting both clarifies the persons meaning and encourages continued conversation.

E: Elicit more. Respond with particular interest and ask for elaboration. "What else?" "In what ways?" "How else could you do that?"

A: Affirm it. Reinforce transformation talk by offering a simple positive comment. "That sounds like a good idea!" "That's a great point!" "It sounds like you have thought this through!"

D: Describe it. Gather a few statements the other person has expressed and describe, at a deeper level, what you are hearing. Think of this as a reflection on steroids.

When you hear someone's DNA, use READ for an immediate response. But, don't just stop there. When you hear someone's DNA, you must also act upon it long term. Tuck the DNA somewhere in your brain where you can quickly retrieve it; as you are going to use it often in all future conversations with this person.

So, what are the high-level take-aways from this action technique which will lead to sustained improved performance?

1) The more you know another's DNA, the more ready you are to increase and motivate another's performance.

2) Desire, need and aim are three layers of language which lead people to a commitment.

3) There are four easy ways to lead people to talk transformation language.

4) When you hear transformation talk (DNA), you act on it immediately and revisit it often.

Chapter 7

Initiate an Action Plan

"We are all capable of success; we just need to know where the starting and finishing lines are."
Corey Pruitt

It is said that when Michelangelo was creating his famous "David" statue commissioned in 1501, he was asked how he created such an incredible work of art. He responded, "David was always in the marble, I just helped him get out."

The fourth action which will lead to sustained, effective, performance is to initiate an action plan. An action plan is the key element which will bring fourth the outcome. Action planning is what carves the outcome out of the marble of commitment.

Action planning is the process of taking stock in the situation, assessing the current state and formulating a game plan. Action planning is accomplished everyday by executives, business owners, domestic managers, college students and everyone in between. Action planning is a vital element to personal and professional success.

The concept of action planning has received a lot of attention in the past decade. The reason is because of the strength and forward momentum action planning can create. Those who formulate an action plan simply achieve more.

Take a glance over these five principles for effective action planning:

1)   Action planning creates direction. The first principle of action planning is to understand the inherent direction the act of action planning creates. Once there is clearly defined direction, you and your staff will be less likely to be pulled by the whims of today, but pushed by the outcome of what will be.

When I travel for business, I always print out maps from the airport to my hotel...from my hotel to the speaking engagement...and from my hotel back to the airport. I am a map glutton. As you can imagine my excitement with GPS and map apps on my phone. Essentially, action planning is like having a map for success.

Once you have a map, you can visually see the direction you need to take to accomplish your desired outcome, and which avenues will lead you to your outcome the quickest and most efficiently.

"Your direction is more important than your speed."
Richard L. Evans

When I coach people, I share with them that action planning is like a compass. The compass directs the individual to travel in the "right" direction to lead them to their desired location. Action planning points in the direction the individual should go, and prepares the game plan for them to get there.

2) Action planning creates momentum. Action planning not only creates direction, but momentum as well. I like to define momentum as, "continual forward movement with energy, force and drive."

If you ever drive on the highways and roads through the Colorado Rocky Mountains, you will quickly pick up on a theme of street signs that say, "Runaway truck ramps." These signs are referring to ramps full of sand (like a giant sandbox). They are for large trucks which have picked up too much momentum down the roads with steep grades. Their momentum takes them past the point of their brakes being effective, so they have to resort to driving into the runaway truck ramps to slow their speed.

Action planning creates this type of runaway-truck-momentum that cannot be stopped until the sandbox of success is reached.

3)   Action planning creates focus. The third principle piggy-backs on the first two. It seems appropriate to assume that if action planning creates direction and momentum, then a natural byproduct would be focus.

According to Webster's Dictionary, focus is defined as, "any center of activity, attention, etc. producing a clear image; to fix or settle on one thing; to adjust one's eye or a lens so as to make a clear image; to direct one's thoughts or efforts; the starting point of an earthquake."

What a perfect definition of what kind of focus action planning accomplishes. Action planning forces one's attention, adjusts one's thoughts and actions to make a clear image, directs one's thoughts and efforts, and starts an earthquake of successful performance outcomes. Action planning inherently produces determined focus.

Focus provides single-minded-motivation to achieve outcomes.

4)   The four "P's" of action planning. A proper ac-
      tion plan must adhere to the four "P's": Precise,
      practical, performance driven and powerful.

      When creating an action plan, it must be pre-
      cise. A proper action plan will have precision
      in defining what the intended outcome is,
      what the perceived hurdles will be, who will
      be involved, what the steps to achievement
      will be, and a description of the time span of
      achievement.

      Unclear action plans produce unclear produc-
      tion. You can't grow tomatoes from pumpkin
      seeds and you can't get sustained performance
      results from unclear action plans.

      Your action plan should always be practical.
      Big action plans are great, but setting unreal-
      istic action plans will actually have the para-
      doxical effect, and will hamper the motivation
      of your staff. A practical action plan is one that
      challenges, but is not unrealistic that there is
      little chance of accomplishment.

      Your action plan should always be performance
      driven. An effective action plan cannot consist
      of factors one cannot control. A proper action
      plan incorporates all the elements under your
      control, the elements that can be measured
      through performance. Performance driven ac-

tion plans allow for track-able progress, bring light to areas in need of alterations and measure results. Performance driven action plans encourage responsibility of action and outcomes.

One quick way to check if an action plan is performance driven is to filter it through this question: "If the outcome of the action plan is not achieved, can the parties involved blame elements outside of their control?" If you can answer "yes" to this question, your action plan may need some refining.

Lastly, your action plan must be powerful. That is, there must be DNA all over it. The more connected the outcome is to the staffs DNA, the more power the action plan will have. And, the more connected the action plan outcome is to DNA the more ready the staff member will be to achieve in spite of the circumstances and opposition surrounding the outcome.

"Obstacles are those frightful things you see when you take your eyes off the goal."
Hannah More

5)   Action plans should empower and not impair. A well-crafted action plan should prove to an employee how much you and the company be-

lieve in them and empower them to be successful at their job.

Empowerment = Productivity
Impairment = Inactivity

Here are eight signs that indicate your staff is not feeling empowered by an action plan:

1) Assignments and tasks are not completed on time
2) Procrastination on projects
3) Errors and mistakes
4) Focus on non-essentials
5) Busy work occupies their time
6) Unsatisfactory output or outcomes
7) Unwilling to ask for help
8) Failure to provide you with timely feedback

Bottom line, empowering action plans increase productivity.

We'll close this technique of performance communication with a few funny, but not so productive, action plan elements.

The Not-So-Productive Employee Action Plan

- I can go anywhere I want if I look serious and carry a clipboard.
- If at first I don't succeed, I will try again... then I will quit. No use being a fool about it.
- Everything can be filed under miscellaneous.

- Never delay the ending of a meeting or the beginning of lunch.
- The last person that was fired or quit will be held responsible for everything that goes wrong...until the next person quits or is fired.
- Always be available for work in the past tense.
- My authority is proportional to the number of pens that I carry.
- When I don't know what to do, walk fast and look concerned.

Chapter 8

Offer Affirmations and Encouragement

"I want to go to work today and be told everything I am doing wrong...I love when people point out all my flaws and short comings...I do hope that happens today at the office!"

I don't know about you, but I don't know too many employees who talk that way. As a matter of fact, I don't know too many humans who talk that way.

Whenever I meet with groups of staff members, in all business sectors, invariably the topic of affirmations surfaces in the conversation. Unfortunately, the topic surfaces as an element that is not being used in the workplace.

I saw a great sign on a colleague's wall that read: "doing a good job here is like wetting your pants in a dark suit...you get a warm feeling but no one else notices."

So often, employees feel that management only notices them when something is wrong. Making an employee feel valued and supported without coddling them is an important balance which fosters improved performance outcomes. Equally important is ensuring that they know they must perform at a high level without making them feel like they have a gun to their head.

This balancing act can be tipped in your favor by using affirmations. Reinforcing the employee's actions when something has gone correctly shows them they are noticed, valued and that management appreciates what they are doing.

G.K.Chesterton, an English Journalist once wrote, "The really great person is the person who makes every person feel great." How would a few words of affirmation change your day? Or your performance? The need for affirmations and encouragement is part of our human make up. Think about the child just learning to walk. She pulls herself up, unsteadily, then smiles a toothless smile, eagerly looking around to see if anyone is watching her amazing ability. As the adoring parents respond with outstretched arms and calls of "come on," she takes a hesitant step. If her effort is rewarded with cheers or a healthy, "good job!" she is more likely to try again until successful.

That need to be affirmed, recognized and encouraged doesn't stop after we learn to walk. Those who have accomplished much, often credit the encouragement of others as a primary factor in their success. Whether a quiet, "I believe in you," or excited cheers from a crowd for "all you've done." No matter what the exterior shows, inwardly we all need that little, "yes you can" push that makes the difference in our lives.

Here is an interesting perspective: every manager, director, VP, chief, etc. will have an influence on those they lead. Whether that influence is helpful or hurtful, positive or negative, depends on whether affirmations and encouragement is used.

They may not always verbalize it, but employees want to be valued for a job well done by those they hold in high esteem.

"People will forget what you said. People will forget what you did. But people will never forget how you made them feel."
Anonymous

Encouragers are special people in our lives. Everyone can quickly name a few of the encouragers in their life. Those encouragers have a quiet self-confidence which allows them to focus on building others up.

The following are five techniques for affirming and encouraging others.

1) Show genuine interest. This is by far the most effective way of affirming and encouraging others. Let others know you care. Express genuine interest by conveying you want to know more about them. Get them to talk about something they are the expert of, themselves.

2) Acknowledge what is important to them. When you acknowledge what's important to others, you provide a form of affirmation and validation about who they are and what they're doing. Whether they admit it or not, each of them craves this acknowledgement deep down.

   This acknowledgement is like a form of expressing understanding of the other person.

When we seek to acknowledge and understand another person it implies a sense of acceptance. And, acceptance leads to respect and open communication.

3)   Respond to one's strengths, efforts and intentions. Often, it is easy to notice the strengths of others. Push your affirmations to the next level and truly look for the efforts people are putting forth, and respond to them. Look for the intentions of others and respond to them.

4)   Say something. When you notice the positive, say so! A simple encouragement can go a long way. These magical words at the right moment can make the difference between "keep going" or "give up" in the other person.

5)   Ask for thoughts and ideas. This is like appropriate flattery. Haven't you felt on top of the world when your peers asked for your thoughts or ideas? Or, when they confided in you regarding an important business decision. This simple act makes them want to help, and do everything to prove that your faith in them was well founded.

"We awaken in others the same attitude of mind we hold toward them."
E. Hubbard

Affirmations and encouragement are critical as you influence action based on your interactions.

Chapter 9

Negotiate Resistance

Growing up, we would play with a little toy called, "Chinese Handcuffs." Every once in a while I see kids can still redeem their game tickets at the local pizza place for Chinese Handcuffs. Chinese Handcuffs are a clever toy in which you place your pointer finger from each hand into each end of a small, flimsy, straw-like tube. Your fingers slide in easily, but pulling your fingers out is a different story. The more you try to pull your fingers out, the tighter the cuff becomes on your fingers. Pulling and pulling does nothing to help you break free from this seemingly easy trap.

The trick to get out of these deceptive claws is to actually push your fingers toward each other. The cuff loosens and you are able to remove your fingers one at a time.

Many of us have learned through the nerve-racking and tear-jerking experience of Chinese Handcuffs, that meeting resistance with resistance doesn't free us.

As adults, sometimes we manage employees by putting one finger in the cuff and forcing the employee to put their finger in the other end. As decisions are discussed, evaluations are expressed, and performance is critiqued, you both attempt to pull your finger out, only to realize the cuff getting tighter. And, the more you both pull the tighter it gets.

The last technique of performance communication is the concept of negotiating resistance. In simpler terms, not getting your finger stuck in the cuff in the first place.

Resistance is an observable behavior that is a warning sign there is conflict in the communication process that needs to change. Resistance is a strong predictor of performance outcomes. The least desirable position for a manager to be in is arguing for a particular behavior or outcome while the staff member argues against it. By simply reducing resistance, you increase the chance of a good performance outcome.

Employees exhibit resistant behavior for a number of reasons. Take a look at a few of these reasons, and a few suggestions to lessen the resistance.

Manager Approach

One of the biggest influencers of resistance, and one of the easiest to fix, is your conversational approach. Your approach can either increase or decrease employee resistance.

Here are two suggestions you may find helpful to ensure your approach is decreasing employee resistance.

1)   Ensure you are being collaborative. The opposite of collaborative is: confronting, nagging,

talking down, criticizing, shaming, blaming, and exerting authority.

To ensure you are being collaborative, actively seek your employee's ideas, suggestions and knowledge. Avoid the need to explicitly express you're the expert and allow your employees to be a part of decisions that involve them.

2) Avoid these common traps:
   a. Question / Answer trap (You ask...they answer...you ask...they answer...)
   b. Information overload trap
   c. Need to fix it trap (Just telling what needs to happen to fix it)

Feeling Lack of Control or Lack of Choice

Many people become agitated, frustrated or resistant when they feel that control and choice have been taken from them. Effective managers and leaders are able to balance their authority and their employee's autonomy.

Here are two suggestions you may find helpful to ensure you are not fostering resistance through squelching control or choice.

1) Avoid directing by giving orders, commands or imperatives. That means, staying away from the "you should..." and the "you need to..." language.

2)   Ask permission first. This helps with the question that is going through your head, right now, from point number one, "What if my staff really does need to do something specific? Very simple, ask permission first.

Ask permission before giving advice, information and suggestions. Here is an example of this powerful suggestion: "Jim, may I share with you an observation? I have noticed that some of your reports have errors in them. Others have found that...(insert suggestions)...I'm wondering what you feel would work for you?"

Let's quickly break down why this is so powerful.

Part I—"Jim, may I share with you an observation?" You are instantly asking permission, which gives Jim the sense of control and choice. It also adds to your credibility and builds rapport.

Part II—"I have noticed that..." Here you very succinctly express your observation. Notice you did not speculate as to reasons for the behavior, you merely expressed what was observable.

Part III—"Others have found..." Now, you are able to offer your suggestion. However, notice how you clothed the suggestion. You put the behavior you observed in the context of—it has happened before and others have done…—This phrasing, or manner of clothing your suggestions, normalize the behavior and allows the other person a different perspective. One major note here: be sure to offer at least two solutions. Remember, you are reducing resistance by adding choice.

Part IV—"I'm wondering what you feel would work for you?" You close by allowing them to express their thoughts on the matter. But, notice you are very specific on where you want them to go…toward a solution…through your question.

Follow this process and you may find it much easier to reduce resistance and add control and choice.

When you find yourself and an employee with your fingers stuck in a Chinese Handcuff, ask yourself the following questions to help you negotiate the resistance:

1) How has my approach / style increased this employees resistance?

2) How can I repackage my suggestions and observations to add an element of control and choice for this resistant employee?

This technique rounds out our six performance communication techniques. If you choose to use these six techniques, you will increase the likelihood that action will stem from your interaction. Here they are one more time:

-   Assess Motivation
-   Connect to DNA
-   Transformation Talk—DNA
-   Initiate an Action Plan
-   Offer Affirmations and Encouragement
-   Negotiate Resistance

"Good leaders make people feel that they're at the very heart of things, not at the periphery. Everyone feels that he or she makes a difference to the success of the organization. When that happens people feel centered and that gives their work meaning."
Warren G. Bennis

Chapter 10

Structure of Performance Communication Session

We have covered a lot of ground up to this point. We started our time together discussing the goals of performance communication:

1) Improve awareness
2) Intensify responsibility
3) Impact behavior change
4) Increase performance

We then moved onto the pillars of performance communication:

- Listening
- Open-questions
- Offer options
- Preferences language
- Support self-efficacy

After that, we rounded out our foundation by chatting about the techniques of performance communication:

- Assess motivation
- Connect to DNA
- Transformation talk, DNA
- Initiate an action plan
- Offer affirmations and encouragement

- Negotiate resistance

We will close our time together by taking a look at seven elements to include into any performance communication session. This portion of the book marks a transition from information to application as we will not only take a look at what the elements are, but also the strategic order in which to use them for maximum impact on performance outcomes.

Performance communication is deceptively simple, yet difficult to master. For this reason, I have outlined the structure as a guide while you work to become proficient at using performance communication in your management and leadership style.

The structure of performance communication is not meant to be a lengthy process, yet a more effective process and a more efficient process as it relates to time. The structure of performance communication is meant to create an environment where performance feedback is shared and accepted in a collaborative manner with buy-in from all parties and with the end result being improved performance outcomes.

The structure of performance communication is not a once-a-year (come review time) method of communication. Rather, it is a daily method of communication feedback which will reap incredible performance results. That is, action from interaction.

I was conducting a seminar when a question was brought to the group about how to handle the employee who violates company dress code and mismanages company time. We worked through the scenario using the structure of performance communication. But, on a break that followed, one of the attendees sent me this email.

Memo from Management—Dress Code and Company Time

Dress Code:

1) You are advised to come to work dressed to your salary.

2) If we see you wearing high end designer clothing, we will assume you are doing well financially, and therefore do not need a raise.

3) If you dress poorly, you need to manage your money better, so you can buy nicer clothes and therefore, you do not need a raise.

4) If you dress just right, you are right where you need to be and therefore you do not need a raise.

Company Time:

1) Sick days: we will no longer accept doctor's statements as proof of sickness. If you are able to go to the doctor, you are able to come to work.

2) Personal days: each employee receives 104 personal days a year. They are called Saturdays and Sundays.

3) Bathroom breaks: Entirely too much time is being spent on the toilet. There is now a strict three minute time limit in the stalls. At the

end of three minutes an alarm will sound, the toilet paper will retract, the stall door will open, and a picture will be taken. Please note anyone caught smiling in the picture will be sanctioned under the company's mental health policy.

Thank you for your loyalty to our company. We are here to provide a positive employment experience. Therefore, all questions, comments, concerns, complaints and input should be directed elsewhere.

Sincerely,

The Management

Although extremely funny, this company memo does not follow the structure of performance communication. The elements in the structure of performance communication are:

1) Initiate session goals
2) Menu of options
3) Probe for knowledge, reality and ownership
4) Request permission
5) Offer feedback
6) View options for correction and improvement
7) Elicit commitment and will

These seven elements create the acronym, IMPROVE. Let's unpack each element and look at a few scenarios.

Chapter 11

Initiate Session Goal and Menu of Options

The first few sentences out of your mouth are so important to increasing performance. The first few moments in the interaction can either deepen performance or destroy performance. The first few phrases set the tone for the rest of the interaction.

The benefits of starting your session by initiating your session goals and using a menu of options are many. Here is a quick list of a few:
- Sets the tone
- Strengthens rapport
- Clarifies expectations
- Communicates respect
- Demonstrates open communication
- Demonstrates collaboration
- Increases comfort level
- Sets the focus
- Avoids meandering
- Makes time more efficient

Take a look at this example of an unsuccessful start:

Manager: "Jim, we need to talk about your sales numbers. They are tanking fast. We have 30 minutes to get this figured out."

Jim: "Ok."

Now contrast that with a successful start to a performance communication interaction.

Manager: "Jim, thanks for meeting with me. I show we have 30 minutes scheduled today. I was thinking we could focus on a few things during our time: your talk time on the phone, your sales numbers and the yearly compliance training. Which of these would you like to talk about first, or is there something more pressing you would like to address first?"

Jim: "Well, I guess we could talk about my sales numbers or my talk time, I would imagine they are linked in some way anyhow."

Manager: "Great Jim! Sounds like this is something you've been thinking about. Regarding your sales numbers and talk time, when we are done chatting today, what do you want to take away from our conversation?"

Time out! Let's break down the crucial pieces in the interactions.

In the first interaction, the manager did two things that could potentially hamper the performance of the employee. First, the manager spoke in imperative language, "we need..." Imperative language is not motivating language when it comes from the mouth of the manager or leader. This manager would benefit from getting some DNA out of this employee first, and then attach the company need to that specific DNA.

Second, the manager made a judgmental interpretation of the employee's performance, "your sales numbers are tanking fast." When the manager interprets performance, it frees the employee from having to interpret the performance, thus taking away a moment of responsibility from the employee.

One thing this first manager did well, he addressed the time frame of the meeting. This added a little more structure to the interaction.

In the second interaction, the manager took full advantage of the first few moments to set the groundwork for improved performance communication.

Take a look:

-       Affirmed—"Jim, thanks for meeting with me." This action sets a warmer, more collaborative tone.

-       Set the time parameter—"I show we have 30 minutes scheduled today..."

-       Provided a menu of options for focus points, "...we could focus on a few things...your talk time on the phone, sales numbers, yearly compliance training. Which of these would you like to talk about first?" Menu of options gives that sense of choice which leads to increased responsibility within the employee.

-       Provided an alternative choice, "...or is there something more pressing you would like to address first?" This allows the employee one more chance to put something on the table, which creates even a greater sense of collaboration.

After Jim's reply, our manager uses one more element. The manager asks for a session goal on the focus area, "...when we are done chatting today, what do you want to take away from our conversation?" This simple act emphasizes the employee's involvement and collaboration in the outcome. This simple question begins to elicit the employees DNA.

Notice the difference in the interaction and we have only just begun. However, we have very quickly increased the chance of improved performance stemming from our interactions.

So what are the key elements in initiating a session goal and offering a menu of options?
1)   Affirmations
2)   Set the time frame
3)   Provide options
4)   Provide an alternative

How you start will have a decisive impact on how you finish. Be sure to incorporate these key elements while initiating your session goal and offering your menu of options.

Chapter 12

Probe for Knowledge, Reality and Ownership

When managing and leading others, there is a temptation for doing most of the talking because, let's face it, you have plenty to say. However, in order to improve awareness, intensify responsibility, impact behavior change and increase performance, we must elicit more than we impose...probe more than we profess...listen more than we lecture.

This portion in the performance communication structure is all about probing for the other person's knowledge, perspective of reality and ownership. Your objectives here are twofold:

1) To catch as much information as possible to help you determine what specific areas your employee can leverage to achieve results.

2) To get your employee to talk themselves into sustained action (transformation talk).

Action from interaction can be enhanced by improving various aspects of the information exchange process. How information is communicated to your employees can greatly influence their understanding, commitment and resulting action.

It is easier for you to outline your employee's performance problem, but this does not create the most receptive environment. In order to gain acceptance of the problem it is best to use probing to let the employee come to the realization themselves. The realization of the problem marks the starting point, and also serves as a marker on the performance continuum.

Probing is all about asking great open-ended questions that will allow your employee to increase awareness, intensify responsibility and increase performance.

One of the most effective, and more neglected, tools of feedback is self-discovery. This is highly effective in increasing awareness and responsibility. Employees are most often aware of areas in need of improvement. The best way for you to incorporate self-discovery is to create a conversational and collaborative environment. In this situation you will ask the employee for opinions, thoughts, ideas, concerns, etc.

Here are some great probing questions that elicit knowledge, reality and ownership:

- What do you already know about_____?
- Regarding _____ what have you been thinking about?
- When it comes to _____ what would you most like to change?
- What have you already thought about _____?
- What would you like to know more about regarding _____?
- Regarding _____ what goals are you working on right now?

- Regarding _____ where are you in relation to your goals?
- What do you think is keeping you from your goals?
- The company expectations are _____, your numbers reflect _____, what do you make of those numbers?
- What is, from your perspective, happening with _____?
- How often is this happening?
- What action have you taken on this so far?

Notice all these sample questions begin with "what" or "how" and not "why", "when" or "who." If your goal is to increase responsibility and ownership, "what" and "how" questions help focus on solutions and action. "Why," "when" and "who" questions lead people toward blame and scapegoats.

Another way to think about probing questions:
- Brainstorming questions start with "what" or "how."
- Blamestorming questions start with "why", "when" and "who."

Involving your employees is easy if you are willing to ask questions, listen and guide your employees to where they are in their performance.

Clearly, there are many benefits to shift from an "I tell you" philosophy to a probing "you tell me" philosophy. Here are few:
- Your staff will feel more empowered
- Your staff will be more receptive
- Your staff will take more ownership

- Your staff will improve individual performance
- Your staff will take on responsibility
- Your staff will increase overall team performance

The bottom line is, when you use the probing technique your employee accepts, chooses and takes responsibility for their thoughts and actions—their commitment to their thoughts and actions rises and so does their performance.

Chapter 13

Request Permission

When I was in undergrad school I interned in the sports department at one of the local news stations. I had a media badge which allowed me special access to areas other people could not go. This badge was my permission to get into interview rooms, locker rooms and courtside.

In performance communication, there are portions of the conversation that need a special badge to have access, to have permission. But, there is a simple way to gain access, to get the permission badge. That simple way is to ask for it.

If your goal is for your staff to improve performance for the long run, and take responsibility for current and future actions, then here is a simple rule of thumb: before giving advice, offering information or sharing feedback, ask permission first.

Though odd for supervisors, managers or leaders to ask permission, this simple conversational decision has a huge impact on performance. The reason: it gives a sense of control and collaboration to your employees. This, in turn, gives them a sense of responsibility and ownership.

Here are a few examples of ways to ask permission:
- If you're interested, I have an idea for you to consider…
- Do you mind if I share my concern?
- May I share some information with you?
- Is it ok if I share an observation with you?
- I'd like to give you some feedback about _____, is that ok with you?

Asking for permission is your all access badge to areas of a conversation you would otherwise not be accessing. Don't forget this simple rule of thumb: Before giving advice, offering information or sharing feedback, first ask permission.

Chapter 14

Offer Feedback

Up to this point in your performance communication session you have initiated a session goal; provided a menu of options; probed for knowledge, reality and ownership; and requested permission to share your own information, observations and advice. Now it's your turn to offer feedback that will improve performance.

Take a look at a few not-so-inspiring feedback statements about employees:

- Works well when under constant supervision and cornered like a rat in a trap.
- When she opens her mouth, it seems that this is only to change whichever foot was previously in there.
- This employee has delusions of adequacy.
- She sets low personal standards and then consistently fails to achieve them.
- This employee should go far...and the sooner he starts the better.
- I will always cherish the initial misconceptions I had of him.

Though many in a leadership position have wanted to say a few of these things out loud, true performance feedback contains a few key ingredients.

1)   Based on observables
2)   Specific to issue and behaviors
3)   Used to develop discrepancy of DNA
4)   Couched with normalizations
5)   Always followed by an exploration of options

Let's quickly unpack these five performance feedback ingredients.

Based On Observables

Performance feedback must be expressed about that which is observable. "Lately, I have noticed..." or "What I have observed is..." or "Others have mentioned they saw..." or "The reports are indicating..." All of these are ways to approach an observable performance feedback issue.

The advantage of keeping your feedback to observables is that it lowers defenses because it does not impose a judgment, and observables are much easier to measure progress in performance if you start with something that is observable.

Specific To Issues And Behaviors

General feedback will result in mediocre performance outcomes. Specific feedback will result in specific performance outcomes. Effective feedback is always specific and always focuses on a specific behavior. It does not focus on the person or the intention, but the observable and specific behavior.

Think of it this way, if you provide feedback that is focused on the individual or his intentions, then you have taken it upon yourself to interpret and judge, rather than focusing on the behavior, which is the realm where the individual can do something about it and take ownership of it. Without the specifics you are left with praise or criticism. Both are based on feeling and judgment and not grounded in improving performance.

Effective performance feedback is always specific and focused on actions and behavior in which performance can improve based on new or different actions and behaviors.

Used To Develop Discrepancy of DNA

Effective performance feedback should guide people in understanding where they stand in relation to the expectations of the company as well as where their current behaviors are not matching with their DNA (desires, needs, aims).

There are many psychological studies that prove people are motivated to make a change and improve performance when they perceive a discrepancy between where they are and where they want to be. This subtle connection between current behavior and performance and the employee's DNA is a huge component in the effectiveness of feedback.

Couched With Normalizations

The fourth ingredient in effective performance feedback is all about how you package your information. Again, we will draw from the field of psychology and use an approach termed normalizing. Normalizing is the act of putting the behavior in a larger context. It is expressing that others have done the same thing. Normalizing builds rapport and decreases the defenses of the other person. Examples help drive this ingredient home, take a look:

- When others have done this, they typically found...
- What's generally recommended is...
- Folks have found...
- Studies have shown...
- Research suggests...

Notice the power in normalizations? They help the other person save face and subtly encourage a realistic view of the actions and the outcomes.

Always Followed By An Exploration Of Options

The fifth, and final aspect of feedback just happens to be the sixth element in the structure of performance communication. So, let's go there now.

Chapter 15

View Options for Correction and Improvement

Now, you are at a power point in your performance communication session. You are at a point where ownership, responsibility, action, empowerment and choice collide. It is time to generate a list of options to help solve the issue, change the behavior and increase performance.

Here is the rub; this list of options is a joint effort, a collaborative list of both the employee's ideas and yours. If you come to the conversation only with your ideas and do not elicit the ideas of your employee, then all the effort up to this point has been in vain. This is where the blame game comes into play. If you give the advice and your employee takes the action and it fails, what will your employee do? Blame you, of course. This is a clear indication of where they see the responsibility lies.

First, get your employee to generate options, then add yours to the pile. If you've played your cards right up to this point, odds are your employee will express many of the options that you were going to say anyway. And, that is more powerful for sustainable performance improvement.

Here are a few ways to get this part of the performance communication session rolling:

- What are some options to help you with _____?
- What are some ways you've already considered to _____?
- What else could you do?
- What if (this or that) constraint were removed?
- If you were to solve this, what would you do first? Second? Etc…
- Considering options, I wonder what makes sense to you?

One last note about this part of the conversation: don't judge or critique the ideas generated by your employee. As a rule of thumb, never judge a thoughtful decision. You can coach and counsel to see both the positives and negatives of the idea, but it is not for you to judge at this point. Remember, it is all about ownership at this point.

Chapter 16

Elicit Commitment and Will

Your performance communication has finally brought you to the point of action, the moment of commitment. You started your conversation by initiating a session goal...you offered a menu of options...you probed for knowledge, reality and ownership...you requested permission and then offered feedback...you then generated a list of options with your staff member...now you are ready to elicit a commitment and a will.

More often than not, as I am analyzing the communication of a company I am consulting, one thing is glaring: many staff do not feel confident that they know what management and leadership want them to do.

Here are ten signs your employees don't know what you want them to do following a feedback session:
1) Assignments are not completed on time
2) Procrastination on projects
3) Errors and mistakes
4) A focus on non-essentials and busy work
5) Unsatisfactory output and outcomes
6) Unwillingness to ask for help
7) Continuously ask for your permission
8) Continuously seek your approval on tasks

9)   Become defensive quickly regarding their work
10) Expectations are not met

So, here is the money statement: a feedback session should never end without some specific commitment and plan of action.

Your goal is action from interaction, so don't gloss over this critical phase of the conversation.

Here are a few suggestions to elicit a commitment:
-   What do you think about this information?
-   Based on this information, what do you see yourself doing?
-   Where does this leave you now?
-   What are the positives and negatives of each option?
-   Where do you go from here?
-   What do you think you'll do?
-   What's the next step?
-   What are you willing to do?
-   What's your action plan?

As your employee begins to express his commitment, be sure to use your listening techniques to draw more out of him. And, be sure to attach his commitment to his DNA for a powerful resulting action.

There you have it, the seven ingredients of the structure of a performance communication session. As you move through the session, be mindful of the techniques of performance communication, the pillars of performance communication, and the goals of performance communication.

Chapter 17

Putting it all Together

"Good management consists of showing average people how to do the work of superior people."
John D. Rockefeller

A man came across a genie. The genie granted the man one wish. The man thought for a second and then said, "I wish to have a bridge from Los Angeles to Fiji so I can travel there whenever I want." The genie quickly replied, "That's nearly impossible. That is thousands of miles of bridge. You would need gas stations, hotels and restaurants along the way. That is just not going to work." The man replied, "Ok, can you help me understand what my employees are thinking?" The genie replied, "How many lanes do you want on the bridge?"

The previous pages uncovered the structure, philosophy and bridge to truly understanding your employees. Better yet, not just understanding them, but to motivate them and impact overall performance improvement.

Commitment Time

So, what are you going to do with all this information? If you are like me you may have highlighted some things, or jotted down some quick "take-aways." But, what are you really going to do with this information?

"Hold yourself responsible for a higher standard than anyone else expects of you."
Henry Ward Beecher

Here is a quick three-step formula to help you commit to the principles, methods and philosophy you read about.

1) Identify your unproductive management communication habits

   If you were to continue on as you have been, what would be the consequences? If you were to make some small changes here and there, what would be the benefit?

   Carefully define what is working and what is not working. What areas are you having the biggest victories and which areas are you having the poorest results?

2) Define your new successful management communication habits

   Life will always give you outcomes related to your actions. Before you start down this new path, define what success will look like for you.

Which principles will you focus on first? Upon which part of the structure will you concentrate your efforts?

What will the payoff be for this new habit? Even during those times when the "new" habit feels uncomfortable, why will you continue on?

3) Create an action plan

Start with three easy steps you will take to ensure the formation of this new habit. What will it take for you to start this new communication habit and what will it take for you to sustain this habit?

Understanding, motivating and improving performance is no small effort. However, the importance of motivation in any workplace is clear to see. Without motivated employees, any manager and leader will find it a lot harder to get desired results.

"If you keep on doing what you've always done, you'll keep on getting what you've always got."
Jack Canfield

Practice using every element of the performance communication philosophy and over time your comfort will grow and your employees will excel with sustainable performance.

Zig Zigler once said, "People often say that motivation doesn't last. Well, neither does bathing—that's why we recommend it daily." Performance communication is a daily practice, it is a daily habit. And, in the end, you will be ecstatic with the results you reap.

Quick Reference Guide

The goals of performance communication:

1) Improve awareness
2) Intensify responsibility
3) Impact behavior change
4) Increase performance

The pillars of performance communication:

1) Listening
2) Open-questions
3) Offer options
4) Preferences language
5) Support self-efficacy

The techniques of performance communication:

1) Assess motivation
2) Connect to DNA
3) Transformation talk, DNA
4) Initiate an action plan
5) Offer affirmations and empathy
6) Negotiate resistance

The structure of performance communication:

1) Initiate session goals
2) Menu of options
3) Probe for knowledge, reality and ownership
4) Request permission
5) Offer feedback
6) View options for correction and improvement
7) Elicit commitment and will

CERTIFIED PERFORMANCE COMMUNICATOR DESIGNATION

Gain fresh ideas...powerful insights...and amazing new techniques for effectively leading your team to new, unparalleled levels of performance through the Certified Performance Communicator designation!

The best step you can make today to be a more effective leader is to build your performance communication skills! Attend this certification and increase your knowledge of:

-   Taking your employees' skills to the next level through performance communication
-   Solving the recurring human capital problems you face as a leader
-   Learning how you can adapt your approach for better results
-   Increasing staff initiative, ownership and responsibility
-   Coaching a team of motivated, productive winners

- Making your staff feel valued, appreciated and understood
- Inspiring performance through effective feedback
- Increasing your leadership effectiveness through communication
- Leading your team to achieve extraordinary and sustainable performance

Who Should Get Certified as a Certified Performance Communicator:

- Business owners
- Chief Leaders
- Directors
- Managers and supervisors
- Team leaders
- Anyone in a position of authority who wants to get better leadership results

Learn more about the Certified Performance Communicator designation at: www.NHCIonline.com

CERTIFIED MASTER COMMUNICATOR DESIGNATION

Research shows the primary skill that differentiates professional success is one's ability to communicate. We all communicate, but this expertise needs to be developed, honed and added to on an on-going basis.

Excellent interpersonal communication skills are the most potent career and personal skills you can possess. Learn how to communicate effectively and confidently with these practical and proven techniques and skills that are essential for executive leadership, managers, supervisors, team leaders and anyone interested in heading for the top!

The Certified Master Communicator has obtained a prowess in:

- *Introduction to Strategic Communication -*
    - o The foundation for effective communication
    - o How eight communication elements impact your effectiveness

- o Four techniques to explode your listening potential
- o Critical listening traps to avoid if you want to be effective
- *Professional Communication Strategies -*
  - o Presentation excellence, meeting management, multi-level corporate communication
  - o The 5 P's of a perfect presentation
  - o Ways to quickly engage your listeners for any presentation
  - o Sure fire techniques for maximum presentation impact
  - o Critical action items to do prior, during and after a meeting
- *Relational Communication Strategies -*
  - o Six ways to instantly connect with anyone
  - o Six steps to engage and retain others in conversation
  - o Never-fail conversation techniques
  - o Seven ways to make your conversation a success
  - o Seven ways to kill any communication situation
- *Conflict Communication Strategies -*
  - o How to quickly recognize conflict styles
  - o The best strategy to manage and resolve conflict
  - o How to motivate in the midst of conflict

Earn the right to promote yourself to Certified Master Communicator and add to your professional skills the invaluable ability to be effective in all communication settings.

Learn more about the Certified Master Communicator designation at: www.NHCIonline.com

ABOUT THE AUTHOR

Corey Pruitt is an innovator specializing in professional development in the areas of communication, motivation and performance improvement. He excels at connecting knowledge with tools to help people be more effective in their particular business realms.

Corey's unique blend of experiences in human behavior, psychology and business:
- As a Therapist/Counselor
- Psychology Professor
- Motivation/Performance Expert and Consultant
- Director of Training/Curriculum Design
- Communications Professor
- Business owner

Have set the foundation for his ability to motivate and educate people toward positive professional growth and lasting performance improvement across all markets and industries.

Corey has obtained an undergraduate degree in Human Communication and a Master's degree in Psychology. He also holds the following certifications:

- Certified in Advanced Motivational Interviewing & Behavior Change
- Certified Master Communicator
- Certified Performance Communicator

Corey has received numerous awards and recognition for his speaking, training and entertaining abilities. He is an established author, as well as the founder and owner of multiple companies.

To book Corey Pruitt for speaking or consulting, email: information@nhcionline.com or call 1-800-965-7636